Slam Dunk

Contents

Shooting hoops	2
A sporting invention	4
The court	6
How to play	7
Offence and defence	8
Rules	10
Scoring points	12
Players in position	14
Player profiles	16
Glossary	21
Basketball moves	22

Written by Rachel Russ

Collins

Shooting hoops

Basketball is a fast-paced game where players **dribble**, pass, dodge, jump and shoot.

Fun fact

A slam dunk is when a player thrusts the ball down through the basket.

Discover everything you need to know before you shoot some hoops!

Fun fact

Some players can soar more than 120 cm into the air. That's high!

A sporting invention

In 1891, James Naismith, a Physical Education teacher from North America, wanted a game that could be played inside throughout the freezing winters.

James Naismith climbed a ladder and nailed two peach baskets to the walls of a gym hall. Then he got a football to throw through them. Basketball was born!

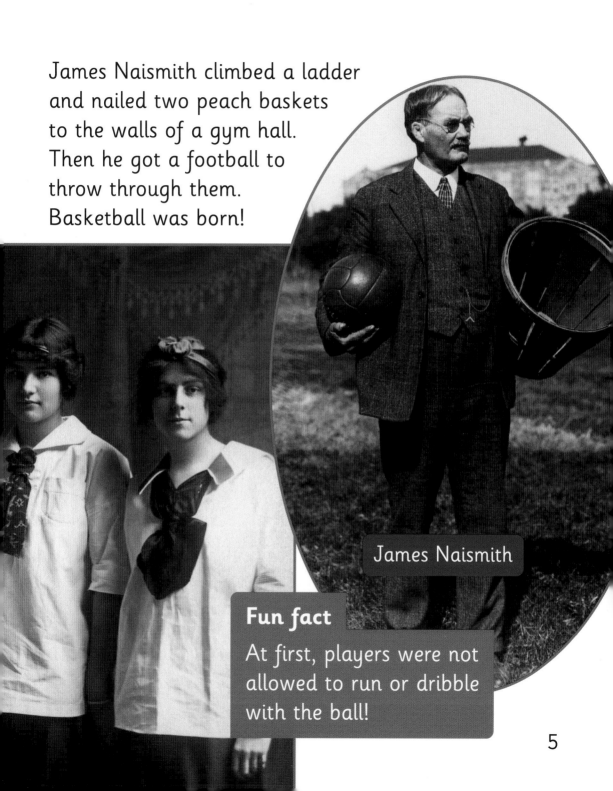

James Naismith

Fun fact
At first, players were not allowed to run or dribble with the ball!

The court

A basketball **court** is divided into two by the midcourt line. Each team has one half of the court.

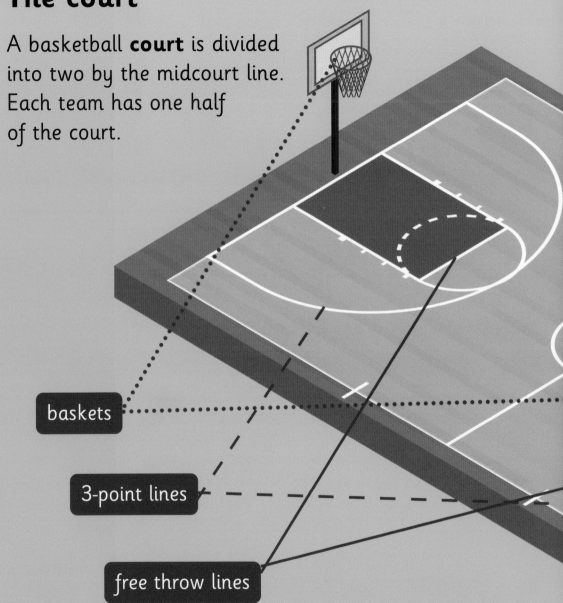

baskets

3-point lines

free throw lines

How to play

In basketball, the players are in two opposing teams. They score points by shooting the ball through the other team's basket.

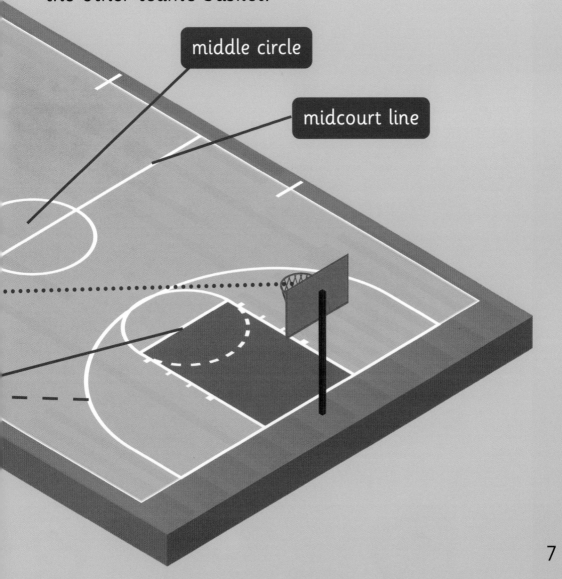

middle circle

midcourt line

Offence and defence

The team in **possession** of the ball is called the offence. They try to score.

The other team, called the defence, must protect their basket. They try to take possession of the ball.

The offence move the ball around the court by dribbling, passing to team-mates or shooting.

Rules

Here are a few rules to know:

- If you dribble the ball past the midcourt line, you cannot return to your own half.

- If you stop dribbling and hold the ball, you cannot start dribbling again.
- When you stop dribbling, you can take two steps to pass, or shoot.

Scoring points

When a player scores, they earn:

-  two points if they are inside the 3-point line
- three points if they are outside the 3-point line
- one point for a free throw.

The team with the most points wins!

Players in position

Each player plays a different position on the court.

There are usually five players on a court and more players on the bench. The coach can make a **substitution** by replacing a player on the court with one from the bench.

15

Player profiles

Jordan

• Jordan jumped so high he looked weightless! His highest vertical leap was over 121 cm!

• He could score from long range and close shots.

• People say he is the greatest player of all time.

Breanna Stewart

• She won two Olympic gold medals with the US team.

• As a child, Breanna dribbled the ball for 1 mile every day.

• In 2011, Breanna was named USA Basketball Female Athlete of the Year.

Bo Kramer

- At 18, Bo was one of the youngest players at the 2016 Paralympics.

- She was the top scorer in the Dutch team who won gold at the Tokyo 2020 Paralympics.

- Bo used big bags of split peas for weight training!

Basketball is one of the most popular sports in the world to play and watch.

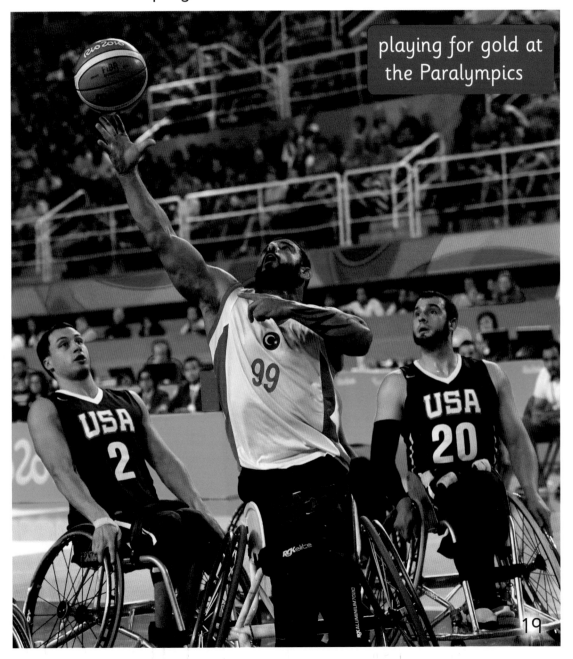

playing for gold at the Paralympics

Why don't you join in the excitement and shoot some hoops in your local park?

20

Glossary

court place you play basketball

dribble bouncing the ball on the floor and walking or running at the same time

long range long distance

possession to have or to own something

substitution changing one player for another player

Basketball moves

dribbling

defending

shooting

scoring

passing

❧ Review: After reading ❧

Use your assessment from hearing the children read to choose any GPCs, words or tricky words that need additional practice.

Read 1: Decoding

- Focus on /ai/ and /sh/ sounds. Ask the children to:
  - read page 16 and find words with two spellings of /ai/ (**weightless**, **greatest**)
  - read the Glossary, and find words showing two spellings of /sh/. (**possession**, **substitution**)
- Challenge the children to pick a page to read aloud fluently, blending any less familiar words in their heads silently.

Read 2: Prosody

- Read page 2, modelling how to use emphasis to create variety (e.g. *in the first sentence list*) and drama in the action words (e.g. **thrusts**, **down**).
- Ask the children to read page 3, using emphasis to bring out the action (e.g. *emphasise* **shoot**, **hoops**, **soar**, **high**)

Read 3: Comprehension

- Ask: Do you think this book teaches you how to play basketball? Which pages are the most useful? (e.g. *the court diagram on pages 6 and 7; the rules on pages 10 and 11*)
- Ask: Do you think the title makes the sport sound exciting? Why?
- Point to the phrase **fast-paced** on page 2. Ask: What does this mean? Tell the children to read the whole sentence to check their understanding, before offering a full explanation. (e.g. *it involves lots of speedy body moves*)
- Turn to pages 22 and 23 and set challenges for the children to practise skimming and scanning.
  - Ask the children to pick a picture and caption, and scan the book to find enough information to form a sentence about the action. Remind them to look at the contents page and glossary.
  - Ask the children to read their sentences, and let the rest of the group scan back to check that any facts are correct.
  - Ask the children to look at the player profiles on pages 16 to 18. Tell them to choose one player and read the bullet points looking for a fact about their achievements. Discuss which words they should look out for e.g. medals, won etc.
- Ask the children to think of a more inspirational title for pages 22 and 23. Suggest that they skim back through the book to get a feel for basketball, and how it could be described.